THE
LONDON, BRIGHTON
AND SOUTH COAST
RAILWAY

The magnificent 1889 station at Lewes, one of the finest surviving Victorian junctions, in September 1906 with one of the celebrated Stroudley 'Gladstones', No.193 *Fremantle*, waiting to depart with an Eastbourne train.

THE
LONDON, BRIGHTON
AND SOUTH COAST
RAILWAY

JOHN MINNIS

The
History
Press

First published in 1999 by Tempus Publishing
Reprinted 2007

Reprinted in 2010 by
The History Press
The Mill, Brimscombe Port,
Stroud, Gloucestershire, GL5 2QG
www.thehistorypress.co.uk

British Library Cataloguing in Publication Data.
A catalogue record for this book is available from the British Library.

ISBN 978 0 7524 4319 5

Typesetting and origination by Tempus Publishing Limited
Printed and bound in Great Britain by
Marston Book Services Limited, Didcot

Contents

Introduction

The Brighton Railway – Image and Reality

Brands for cars, food, soft drinks or almost any product we use are all around us. But the introduction of brands is a relatively recent phenomenon dating back to the latter part of the nineteenth century. Almost the first conscious attempts at branding were the railway companies: as the largest and some of the few truly national business entities in the country, they imposed themselves on the public consciousness in a way that few could emulate. The strength of these brands may be seen in the number of people who still express loyalty, at times reminiscent of football supporters, to the old railway companies nearly eighty years after they ceased to exist.

The London, Brighton & South Coast Railway provides a particularly fine example of the success of this creation of a brand. Although geographically and financially a relatively small concern, it attracted a strong and devoted following of enthusiasts in the earliest days of the railway hobby. It had a powerful public identity, enhanced by a showy locomotive livery and strove to promote itself as something glamorous and exclusive. This concept was exemplified in the 'Southern Belle', 'the most luxurious train in the world' and in the all-first class 'City Limited'.

The line served some of the most demanding passengers in the country. Brighton was then a centre of great wealth and the company had perhaps the highest proportion of first class season ticket holders of any British railway. John Pendleton in *Our Railways* of 1896 commented:

> The first-class passenger to Brighton…is generally imperious, and if obliged to brook delay is apt to call the guard, or to demand – especially if he happens to be an Anglo-Indian military officer overheated with curry and chutney and accustomed to somewhat despotic rule – the head of the stationmaster on a salver, consigning the directors meanwhile to a place where the temperature is reputed to be higher than that of the land in which some of Rudyard Kipling's characters pant.

Once it had recovered from the financial crisis to which the actions of its management had largely contributed in the 1860s, the company was well regarded in the financial

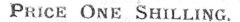
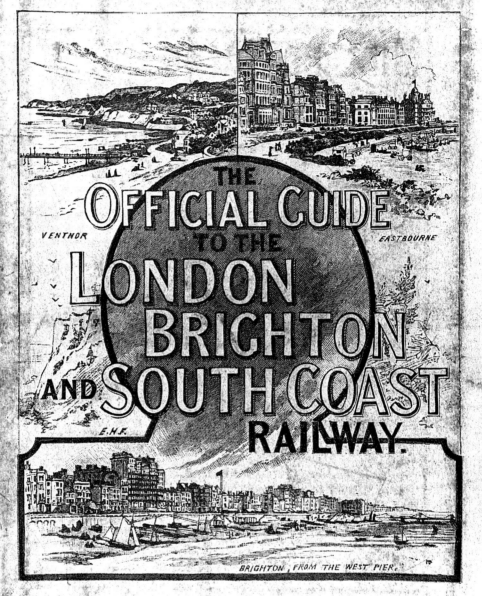

PRICE ONE SHILLING.

(Or Cloth Lettered, 2s.)

THE OFFICIAL GUIDE TO THE LONDON BRIGHTON AND SOUTH COAST RAILWAY.

VENTNOR

EASTBOURNE

BRIGHTON, FROM THE WEST PIER.

CASSELL & COMPANY, LIMITED;

LONDON, PARIS, NEW YORK & MELBOURNE.

The well-known publishers Cassell & Co. published Official Guides for a number of the leading British railway companies, including the Brighton. This edition of 1888 is in paper covers. The guides were also available in a red cloth binding. They were issued at regular intervals over a long period up to the First World War..

world. Financial tipsters praised the LB&SCR's prospects. Among them was W.W. Wall who wrote in his *British Railway Finance: A Guide to Investors* (1902):

> This company has always been a favourite with the railway investor, and there is probably more speculation in 'Berthas', as the deferred shares are called, than in any other deferred shares in the railway list. For one thing, this company has always been well managed, and we have less need to complain of lavish capital expenditure than in the case of the majority of the other railway companies.

Another writer, W.R. Lawson in *The Brighton Railway, its Resources and Prospects* (1891), found that Brighton Deferred stock combined 'the highest return as an investment, with the best prospect of future appreciation and the smallest risk of retrogression.' But appeal to investors does not necessarily mean that service to consumers was of a high standard; paucity of capital expenditure, while a benefit as far as the short term investor was concerned, could mean outdated facilities for passengers. How did the LB&SCR fare in this respect? Great store was set in the 1880s by the handsome and efficient locomotives of William Stroudley, the luxury of the newly-introduced Pullman cars and the generous accommodation afforded by the beautiful stations of T.H. Myres on the recently opened branch lines deep in rural Sussex. The reality of everyday travel on the line may have been less appealing.

Agitation by the residents of the well-to-do South London suburb of Forest Hill for a new station unleashed a torrent of abuse in the local newspaper at the company for the lack of punctuality of its trains and for the often disgusting state of its carriages. The *Forest Hill, Sydenham & Penge Gazette* commented in 1879 that 'it would be difficult to find dirtier or more disgraceful carriages than are found in some of the Brighton Company's trains.' The LB&SCR's success in running excursions had unwanted side-effects as was revealed by a Dr Rendle in a letter to the paper on 27 February the same year:

> How we are annoyed in time of excursion and festival trains, often we find no room for us, our best carriages not unfrequently occupied by doubtful, unclean or rowdy excursionists…Not long since I found that my first class carriage had been the day before the scene of a debauch and a vomit, which had not been cleared away. Often the cloth linings are so saturated with animal odour and stuffiness, that fever in a susceptible person is a result to be expected.

Even assuming that the passenger was not as unlucky as poor Dr Rendle, the lack of speed of many of the trains gave rise to much criticism. The early 1890s saw the East and West Coast companies engaging in what became known as the Railway Race to the North. This prompted *The Times* to devote some editorials to the theme 'The Crawl to the South'. Many express trains failed to manage an average speed of 36mph and when this was combined with what were felt to be exorbitant fares, the reasons for the company's unpopularity are clear. There was one other factor entering into the equation: by 1900, the Brighton was almost unique among British railway companies in continuing to exclude third class passengers from some of its principal expresses. The noted railway economist, William Acworth concluded in his *The Railways of England* (1900): 'In these days of fierce competition between different seaside resorts, it is hardly possible for a Company to pay too dearly in order to purchase a reputation for liberality'.

In seeking to maintain a reputation for exclusivity while providing a less than brilliant service to the majority, it is perhaps little surprise that the LB&SCR, along with its southern neighbours, was proposed as an ideal test case for nationalization in a Fabian Society Tract of 1910. However, by that time, things had moved on. The widening of the main line had done much to improve punctuality, the general standard of passenger accommodation had improved and only the 'City Limited' remained first class only.

Among enthusiasts (or railwayists as they called themselves) the Brighton line was highly regarded. One of the first books to be devoted to the locomotives of an individual company described the history of its engines in detail in 1903, while postcards of its engines were avidly collected and lists of numbers and names were prepared. The fans could even buy photographs of their hero, Mr Stroudley. When the pioneer enthusiast body, the Railway Club, split in 1910, those in the forefront of forming the break away organization, the Stephenson Locomotive Society, G.F. Burtt, L.E. Brailsford, H.T. Buckle and Montague F. Long were all Brighton followers and some, including Burtt, worked at Brighton works. This long standing interest centred on the LB&SCR's locomotives helped create and then perpetuate an image that, as I have suggested, did not always entirely concur with reality.

My intention in this book is to try and show both sides of the LB&SCR: the splendid locomotives appear in profusion in all their glory; However, I have also tried to show something of the variety of the company's services and of its activities. As far as possible, the photographs have not appeared in previous publications. If there is a bias, it is towards the London end of the system as the rural lines have been better covered in recent books and, on the whole, changed less in the course of time.

A surprising proportion of the LB&SCRS's infrastructure still exists. Although there have been some closures of the rural lines, its main lines, suburban routes and coastal branches remain largely intact and the majority of its stations are still in existence. It has probably the highest survival rate in terms of its architecture of any of the pre-1923 companies and some stations, such as Berwick, can display an almost complete set of the buildings that made up a country station: station building, waiting shelter, signal box and railway cottages.

Although locomotives have fared less well, ten per cent of Stroudley's celebrated 'Terriers are still with us and the Bluebell Railway's intention to recreate a Victorian LB&SCR train using carriage bodies that have been rescued from farms and gardens to accompany its two 'Terriers' is an exciting project for the twenty-first century.

For those who would like to know more about the LB&SCR, the Brighton Circle, a society covering all aspects of the history of the railway, was founded in 1974. The Circle produces an excellent journal and membership is highly recommended. Contact may be made through its Secretary, P.J. Wisdom of 76 Woodbourne Avenue, Brighton, East Sussex, BN1 8EJ.

One
London to Brighton

Memorably likened by Hamilton Ellis to a Victorian overmantel, the new Victoria Station of 1909, whose upper floors were used as an annexe to the Grosvenor Hotel, managed to combine the mansards of the French Second Empire style in deference to the adjoining hotel with all the exuberance of Edwardian baroque.

Along with the widening of the main line, the major civil engineering work carried out on the LB&SCR in the twentieth century was the rebuilding of Victoria Station. The new south portion of the station is under construction in this view which also shows the roof of the LC&DR portion in the background.

One of the most notable features of the rebuilt Victoria Station – often unnoticed by travellers – is the splendid screen wall built along Buckingham Palace Road mingling red brick with Portland stone facings. The picture probably dates from 1908, as the station was nearing completion.

Around 1903, one of the well-proportioned Stroudley G Class singles, No.337 *Yarmouth*, leaves the LB&SCR's city terminus, London Bridge, with the overall roof authorized in 1864 prominent in the background. The signals date from the 1880s but have recently received new arms as part of the wholesale modernization carried out from 1898 onwards. The first vehicle is a Stroudley six-wheeled brake van, the lower pitch of the roof contrasting with the Billinton vehicle behind. A Stephenson Clarke loco coal wagon is behind the locomotive. The company held the loco coal contract for the LB&SCR at this time and their wagons were to be seen throughout the system.

An unidentified E4 on a down special goods passing Clapham Junction, c.1902. The West London Extension Railway veers off to the right behind the North signal box which, opened in 1894, had a short life being replaced in 1910 on widening. The impressive groups of tall signals are typical of the LB&SCR in the London area. The photograph was probably taken by A.J. Chisholm.

Widening of much of the Brighton main line was undertaken in the early 1900s with the stretch between Balham and Windmill Bridge Junction quadrupled by 1903. Photographs of the intermediate stations prior to widening are seldom found. Streatham Common is seen looking towards Norbury very much as built in 1862. The all timber canopy with weather screens at each end was rather crude and certainly inadequate for the volume of traffic that had grown up by the time it was replaced.

The widening led to a number of suburban stations being rebuilt on a grand scale. One such was Norbury, rebuilt in 1903 in a 'Free Renaissance' style, fashionable at the turn of the century with its multiplicity of windows, dormers, tall chimneys and use of red brick and tiles in contrast to the stucco and slate favoured a few years earlier. The booking hall was lit by a large circular window high in the gable.

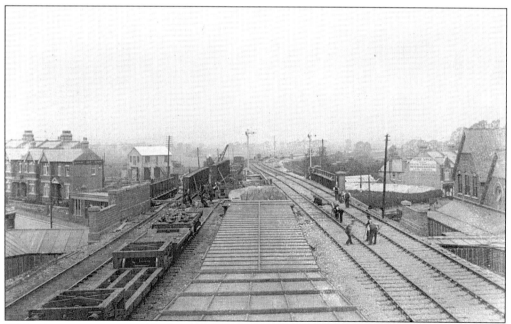

Widening in progress at Norbury in 1903. The new girders for the bridge over London Road are being lowered into position. The new station buildings stand completed on the right.

A five-ton crane removing old girders from the Brigstock Road Bridge following its replacement as part of the widening. The new Thornton Heath Station takes shape in the background. The photograph was taken at 6.30 a.m. on 22 March 1903.

Brockley, looking towards New Cross, c.1900. Opened in 1871, it was the home station of the General Manager, J.P. Knight who owned property in the area. It was totally rebuilt in the early 1970s.

16

Penge was very rarely photographed in pre-grouping days. The down building seen here was built in 1863, identical in design to that at Waddon. It shows evidence of work authorized in 1920 to create a new porters' room. D3 No.377 enters the station with a down local. Photograph by G.H. Cannon.

The suburban setting of Anerley shows how the railway transformed South London. When the London and Croydon Railway (part of whose station is visible surrounded by later work of 1874) was opened, the area was a fashionable resort for Londoners.

East Croydon with Stroudley's G Class single No.329 *Stephenson*. The view is of special interest as it depicts the rebuilding of the station which was carried out between 1896 and 1898 on a grand scale at a cost of over £28,000 for the buildings alone. The new building on the bridge is nearly completed but work on the footbridge and steps has not yet started. For some reason, although it was one of the busiest stations on the LB&SCR and the town of Croydon had many local photographers, East Croydon Station was camera-shy until the turn of the twentieth century. Only one view showing the pre-1897 station is known to exist and that only shows the station as part of a general view of the town taken from the tower of the new town hall.

The completed station building at East Croydon, following the rebuilding of 1896–1898. The station remained largely unchanged until recently when it was swept away and replaced by a striking glass structure. Croydon Corporation Tramways car No.8 passes. The LB&SCR frequently constructed offices for coal merchants at its stations, those seen here being occupied by Moger & Co., Hall & Co., Parry and Rickett Smith, all of whom had a number of depots on the system.

Horley Station as rebuilt a little to the south of its predecessor in 1905. Built in the same neo-Georgian style as the neighbouring station at Earlswood, it projects an image of restrained taste and financial rectitude and its resemblance to many contemporary banks is likely to be no coincidence.

Horley Station photographed between 1890 and 1892 by G.B. Spencer Johnstone. The station building is in part the original London and Brighton Railway structure of 1841 by David Mocatta as enlarged in 1862 by the addition of a second storey containing a flat for the stationmaster. The canopy and footbridge date from 1884 while, in the distance, Horley South signal box of 1875 is visible. The enormous station name-boards favoured by the company at this period are much in evidence. The use by Mocatta of a neo-Jacobean style contrasted with his use of classical or Italianate forms at other London and Brighton stations although each was similar in plan, being early examples of modular design. The extension faithfully reproduced the style of the original portion of the building. After replacement in 1905, the building became the stationmaster's house and survived into the 1960s.

Burgess Hill, an 1877 building located on a road over-bridge, displaying the company's fondness at this time for prominent corbels derived from Venetian gothic originals.

Hassocks, the down side, c.1910. This was the only one of the handsome domestic revival stations designed by T.H. Myres to be situated on a main line. It replaced an early Mocatta structure, which was retained as a cottage, in 1880. All the characteristic features of Myres's work are present: the delightful fretwork porch, the coloured glass, the applied half timbering and the decorated eaves. Sadly, all was demolished in 1973.

The north portal of Clayton Tunnel is one of the best known structures of its type in the country. Famous for the cottage perched between the two towers flanking the tunnel opening, many myths have surrounded it and the purpose for which the cottage was built. The facts are actually more prosaic: the LB&SCR Board authorized a cottage to be built for a signalman in 1849.

A VIEW AT PATCHAM. 1231.

The once beautiful approach to Brighton through the Downs at Patcham – a scene now totally transformed by the building of the Brighton bypass and interchange with the London Road. B4 No.47 on the up 'Southern Belle' has just passed a down train of semi-elliptical roof stock.

Brighton in 1882. An official photograph taken at the time of the re-signalling of the station. Although the image is faded, the new West box and beyond it the massive 240-lever South box built over a siding may be distinguished, while, beyond, the original North box of 1862 is just visible. By the divergence of the line to Hove in the foreground is the clock tower, of which a sketch was approved by the LB&SCR Board on 1 December 1862.

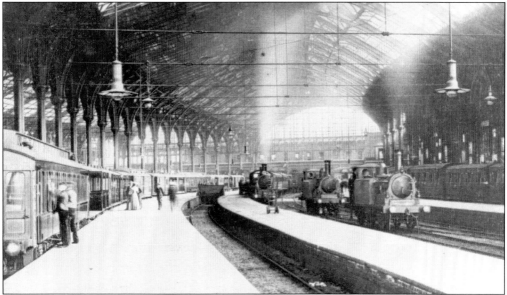

Under the roof of Brighton Station, lit from the outset by electric light (in the use of which the LB&SCR was a pioneer), the 5 p.m. train to Victoria and London Bridge stands on the left in 1901. Also visible are two Pullmans and a Stroudley mail van, one of three built in 1878. Through coaches from Worthing in the centre of the photograph are about to be added to the London train which divided at East Croydon while two D1s await their next duty on the right.

The centre of the LB&SCR's operations, Brighton, *c*.1892. The great iron roof dating from the remodelling of the station in 1882-1884 dominates the view. The west branch platforms on the right serving Hove and the West Coast line were controlled by the 120-lever West signal box of 1881 which was abolished on 16 October 1932 when the main line was re-signalled in conjunction with electrification. The Saxby and Farmer signals were those installed in 1881-1882 and lasted in this form until the turn of the century. All the rolling stock visible is of Stroudley origin. Photograph by G.B. Spencer Johnstone.

Two

Along the Coast

Shoreham by Sea, c.1900, before the slotted post signals were replaced. The station had been rebuilt in 1892 in the stucco style favoured on the coast lines. The West signal box of 1877 on the left lasted until the mid 1980s.

D1 No.80A (the only known view of it bearing this number) approaches Bungalow Town Halt from the east with a four coach motor train on 9 September 1911. The halt had been opened less than a year earlier and bears the inscription 'Alight here for Aerodrome'. As such, it must have been one of the first stations to serve an airport in England, if not the world. Built to serve the extraordinary collection of old carriages and shacks on Shoreham beach, it was later renamed Shoreham Airport. Photograph by H.J. Stretton-Ward.

An E1 on an eastbound cattle train passes Ham Bridge Halt (a motor train halt opened in 1905 and now known as East Worthing) on 21 August 1911. The cattle vans, four Billinton and one Stroudley with the lower pitched roof, are liberally whitewashed to prevent disease and are followed by a Billinton brake van. The halt is surrounded by market gardens and greenhouses for which the Worthing area was once famous and which provided a source of much traffic to the railway. Photograph by H.J. Stretton-Ward.

Angmering, prior to complete rebuilding in 1876. Taken from a damaged albumen print, this photograph has only recently come to light and is the sole known view of the original station which was opened in 1846. This is the up side looking east and the buildings are typical of early coast line stations being built of flint with brick quoins.

The terminus at Littlehampton, in 1910 with the new canopy of the familiar LB&SCR scalloped pattern which replaced the original in 1900-1901. Every conceivable part of the wall of the station building under the canopy is taken up with advertising. Photograph by F.W. Spry, the prominent Littlehampton photographer.

Barnham Junction for the Bognor branch. The old station of 1863 after the new signal box of 1911 was constructed but before the rebuilding of the down platform was completed.

Barnham Junction, c.1912, following completion of the rebuilding of the island platform on the doubling of the branch. The original station building of 1863, replaced in 1936, is visible behind, while the wooden goods shed was of even greater antiquity, having originally been erected at Yapton in 1847 and moved to Barnham in 1864. The seventy-five lever signal box of 1911, extant today, completes the picture.

Bognor Railway Station.

Bognor Station, rebuilt in 1902 after a fire, was typical of the generous provision of accommodation seen in the company's reconstructions of its seaside stations. The LB&SCR devoted much expenditure to this work settling its account with the contractor responsible for the new station, Johnson & Co. Ltd, in 1903 for nearly £91,000. Its style may best be described as eclectic and cheerful, with its tower and variety of fenestration. The wrought iron gates and railings which were an attractive feature were supplied by the Crittall Manufacturing Co. Recently listed, the station has again been affected by fire and repaired.

Level crossings were frequently met with on the coast lines: motor train halts were opened at several of them. Southbourne was one of those, dating from 1906. The crossing keepers house in the background was of a standard design found all along the coast line and dating back to its opening in 1846-1847. Comprising two rooms up and two down, it was dark and cramped. However several similar ones, albeit extended, still survive.

Emsworth showing the reconstruction of the station in 1900. The waiting shed of 1891 remained as did the wooden 1846 goods shed although this was replaced by a corrugated iron structure in 1912. Beyond the new concrete facings for the platforms the 1876 signal box is about to be replaced by a new box.

Havant, *c.*1907. Although facilities were shared with the LSWR, everything in view is of LB&SCR origin. B2 No.317 is on an up passenger train while C2 No.449 is in the yard with a Stroudley brake van and a horsebox. Both engines would be rebuilt with larger Marsh boilers within a few years, No.317 in 1908 and No.449 in 1912. The paired signal posts were much favoured by the Brighton company. Havant East Junction box of 1876 is, following extension by the SR in 1938, still in use today. The station itself, however, was rebuilt by the Southern Railway in their *moderne* style in 1938.

Portsmouth Town *en fête* on an unknown occasion early in the twentieth century, as seen from the high level platforms. The station, used jointly by the LB&SCR and the LSWR, was rebuilt in 1866 in the highly fashionable French Second Empire style with high mansard roofs and copious ironwork.

Second only to the Ouse Valley Viaduct is the striking London Road Viaduct in Brighton. The vast structure is seen looking towards London Road Station with the 'Southern Belle' Pullman set standing in the long-vanished carriage sidings at the end of the viaduct, c.1910.

Lewes Road on the Kemp Town branch. This is one of only two known pre-grouping photos of the station both taken on the occasion of a Congregational Church outing on 5 July 1907. The scene reminds us of how extensive this kind of traffic once was. Although Lewes Road was opened in 1873, the station buildings seen here date from 1894 when the station was completely rebuilt.

In Marsh umber, E5 class No.404 running as a 2-4-2T makes its way through the downland scenery to the west of Lewes in this well composed view by E.S. Hallett, c.1908. Lewes Prison stands on the brow of the hill.

Lewes with D1 No.223 in Marsh umber on a train from Brighton. The leading Billinton brake van is in the attractive but short lived umber and white livery. The rebuilt station of 1889 was and is one of the finest stations in the South East, the great iron and glass roof remaining little changed to this day. A number of cards were issued with the words 'A few lines from Lewes', being a pun on the extensive junctions there.

The view northwards from Newhaven Town in September 1909 showing the large goods shed built on the North Quay in 1901. The crossing keeper's house is unusually slate-hung to keep out the damp in this exposed coastal location.

Newhaven Harbour Station with the line to Seaford branching off to the left and the railway-owned London and Paris Hotel on the right. All that is left of the buildings seen here is the Harbour South box of 1886, the extensive range of passenger sheds succumbing in the early 1970s.

The quayside at Newhaven with the Harbour Station of 1889 in the background. During the 1880s, the LB&SCR spent considerable sums developing its facilities at Newhaven to serve the Dieppe traffic in conjunction with the Harbour Company. Large warehouses with barrel vaulted roofs were constructed and extensive handling equipment provided.

One of the least photographed stations on the Brighton system, Bishopstone, looking towards Newhaven, c.1905. The signal box is believed to date from 1894 and was closed in 1922. The station buildings may charitably be said to be unpretentious. The station was intended to serve residents of the nearby tide mills village on this inhospitable stretch of beach.

The concourse of the magnificent terminus at Eastbourne, one of the company's principal stations. The station was completely rebuilt in 1886 in the form in which it still exists today. The attractive boards at the entrance to the platforms and the luggage registration kiosk are characteristic features of the larger LB&SCR stations.

Polegate, an example of the stucco Italianate style favoured by the company for many stations along the coast between 1864 and 1889. Built in 1881, when the station was resited, it has much in common with the middle class villas of resorts such as St Leonards and Hove with its heavy window hood mouldings and eaves corbels. Pre-1923, the stucco was generally left unpainted giving a drab appearance. The porch was subsequently removed and, following a second resiting of the station in 1986, the building has become a restaurant.

Pevensey and Westham station looking towards Polegate, c.1914. A typical coast line station with its level crossing. The buildings visible dated from the 1892-1893 rebuilding following protests from residents concerning the inadequacy of its predecessor. The footbridge is of standard pattern supplied by H. Young & Co. in 1887.

Another seaside resort to gain a new station was Bexhill which enjoyed a huge growth in population from the 1890s onwards. Although the last rebuilding had only taken place in 1892, a new station was authorized in 1897 and built in 1901. The result was a handsome station with extensive awnings to the platforms, mainly extant, although in poor condition.

Three

Town and Country

The Croydon and Oxted Joint line was built through difficult terrain as may be seen in the many cuttings through the chalk of the North Downs. An I2 tank No.15 passes the SER box at Riddlesdown.

Oxted Station on the joint LB&SCR/SER line opened in 1884. The signal box dated from 1896 and lasted until 1987. The excursion train composed of a Billinton suburban block set is hauled by No.309 *Splugen*; this is one of the few photographs to show a member of this class on a train.

A rural junction on the Kent-Sussex border, Groombridge Junction with the lines to Eridge and Ashurst Junction diverging to the left and right respectively. The signal box was opened in 1880 and closed on 23 November 1958.

The charming station building at Rowfant on the East Grinstead branch, which served the Locker-Lampson estate and had a porch for the family's coachman to await their return. The covered footbridge was added in 1899 and the waiting room the following year as part of a programme of improvements to the station which was opened in 1855 although the station building dated from 1860.

Well known today as part of the Bluebell Railway, Horsted Keynes was a remarkably large junction in the middle of nowhere. Another Myres station with particularly attractive valencing, it is seen from the end loading dock in which is standing an LB&SCR horsebox, its flap down. The date is c.1910.

Horeham Road on the Cuckoo line from Eridge to Polegate, so called because of the ancient Cuckoo Fair held at Heathfield. Looking south, the view is post 1911 as the wagons carry the large lettering introduced that year. The goods yard is full of wagons, mainly Open As. The station appears very trim with its Myres station building which had its original half timbering covered with tiles only ten years after construction in 1880 due to damp penetration. Closed to passengers in 1965, the station was demolished in the 1970s.

The next station northwards on the Cuckoo line, Heathfield's station building still looks much the same today as it did in this pre-1914 view. The new community that grew up around it echoed the style of its architecture in the use of red brick and tiling.

Level Crossing Old Shoreham Bridge. Lancing College in distance   H 30 CLASSI

The level crossing by the Old Shoreham Bridge, a wooden affair of 1781 acquired by the LB&SCR. The sign reads 'This bridge is only capable of carrying the ordinary traffic of the District'. The crossing keeper's house replaced an earlier structure on the site in 1895 and is in the style much favoured by the company for its cottages in the 1880s and early 1890s, often found in pairs. The signal box followed in 1896.

Partridge Green, *c*.1905. Opened in 1861, the station building was similar in style to others on the Shoreham-Horsham line. The signal box is something of a mystery as no date for its construction is given in the official signalling records. The single storey railwaymen's cottages are a rare survival, such structures generally disappearing in the 1880s. Station building, goods shed and cottages were all demolished in the 1970s.

Faygate, looking towards Horsham, *c*.1910. The main station buildings are the originals of 1848 with another room added in 1864 and further extensions to the ground floor in 1897. They were demolished in the 1970s. The waiting shelter dates from 1875 and the signal box from 1877.

Located on the Horsham-Guildford line of 1865, Slinfold was one of the smallest stations on the LB&SCR. Remarkably, it had two signal boxes: in the foreground, the South Box of 1895 (closed in 1933) and in the distance, the North Box that lasted until closure in 1965. A large assortment of trunks is piled up on the platform.

One of the most attractive stretches of the Brighton system within Surrey was the route through the Mole Valley between Leatherhead and Dorking. Here a down train passes the ornate crossing keeper's house at Mickleham Crossing in 1912. It is headed by I1 No.5 and comprises a long line of Stroudley carriages and one of the seldom-photographed diagram 149 outside-framed fish and meat vans.

The up platform at Epsom Town shortly before the station was closed in 1929 and a new station opened on the site of the former LSWR station. The station buildings dated from 1875 and the main building on the down side is still there but the portion seen was removed soon after closure.

Tulse Hill, an important inner London junction opened in 1868. For some reason, it was rarely photographed in pre-grouping days.

Crystal Palace, looking towards Victoria during the transitional period when the overhead electrics were still in use but the third rail was laid in readiness for the new services which commenced in June 1928. The goods shed was constructed in 1864 and lasted into the 1980s. Motor trains fill the bays. The photograph is by the late G.L. Gundry, a great observer of transport in London.

Motor trains became a feature of LB&SCR suburban working in the Edwardian era. D1 No.290 is propelling a single trailer brake on a Sutton-West Croydon service into Waddon Station on 25 August 1912. The station was opened in 1863 and the up platform roof was added in 1895. Complete rebuilding occurred in 1936.

The Wimbledon-West Croydon line had much of the character of a country branch line. Although this view of Morden – c.1908 – by A.F. Selby is from a poor print, it is valuable as the only known photograph to show the signal box opened in 1890 and closed prior to 1914. The station house – c.1857 – was enlarged and the single storey waiting room added in 1889.

Another bucolic scene on the same line: Mitcham in 1912 with D1 No.238 on a rake of Stroudley four wheelers. Allotments tended by railwaymen, once a characteristic sight on suburban routes, complement the natural greenery.

A fine composition beautifully lit by a low sun as H1 No.37 passes Hackbridge with a short up Victoria train at 6.30 p.m. on 31 May 1912. The station had opened with the line in 1868 but the canopies seen here date from a partial rebuilding in 1907. The signal box is of early Saxby and Farmer design dating from 1868. The view gives an excellent impression of a typical small LB&SCR goods yard handling mainly coal and building materials.

Typifying the difficult territory encountered by the company in building many of its suburban lines, this is the deep chalk cutting on the line between Carshalton and Sutton with D1 No.283 on a down train of six wheelers on 26 May 1912.

A down train hauled by D1 No.260 pulls out of Ewell on the Epsom line in July 1912. The small station still stands in a semi-rural location today although the inter-war years saw considerable population growth at Ewell.

Epsom Downs was a source of much revenue for the LB&SCR although the Derby was producing less traffic by 1908, the date of this photograph, than it had thirty years earlier. A race special set of Stroudley first class six wheelers fill one of the nine platforms. Locomotives include E5 No.567 and D3 No.380.

Four

Locomotives: The Craven, Stroudley and Robert Billinton Eras

Photographs of the extraordinary variety of locomotives that appeared during the regime of John Chester Craven, the Locomotive Superintendent from 1847 to 1870, are never easy to find and many of his designs went unrecorded by the camera. We often have to make do with rather poor copies and this extremely rare view of No.133 *Penge* at Brighton shed is one such example. A small 'Jenny Lind' built at Brighton in 1859, it was overhauled by Stroudley and given its name in November 1871. The photo was taken between then and November 1878 when it was renumbered 405 before being withdrawn the following year.

Bearing full Craven livery of Brunswick green with painted number enclosed by a gold leaf scroll, No.147, a large single with 6ft 6in drivers built in 1861 stands at what is believed to be New Cross shed in the late 1860s. The prefabricated corrugated iron building has circular windows of a type seen on the nearby Cold Blow signal works. One of three similar locomotives used on London-Brighton expresses, No.147 was named *Worthing* by Stroudley and lasted until 1886.

Built by Robert Stephenson & Co. in 1864, No.490 was one of twelve engines that used material prepared for an Egyptian Government Railways order that was cancelled. At Battersea shed as modified by Stroudley in 1871, the date is after November 1887 when the engine was renumbered and before March 1890 when it was sent to Tunbridge Wells before scrapping in 1896. Shed indications on the footplate valence were introduced in January 1884 while the wagon A5600 in the background is an early example of the ubiquitous round-ended Open A in light grey with the 'illiterate' mark.

Perhaps the nearest Craven came to a standard passenger class were the thirty 2-4-0s built in batches by Brighton Works, Beyer Peacock and Dubs. Taking water at London Bridge at 3.30 p.m. on 24 June 1893 in this photograph by Dr T.F. Budden is No.461, one of the Dubs batch. Ordered in April 1866, by the time they were ready in December, the Brighton company's financial troubles meant that they had no money to pay for them. Dubs delivered the order to Lillie Bridge sidings, West Brompton where the engines deteriorated in the open and parts were pilfered. They finally reached the LB&SCR in April 1867 and had to be renovated before entering service.

The LB&SCR had twenty-five 0-6-0 goods locomotives broadly similar in design but with many variations in detail. No.250, one of the final batch of six built by Slaughter & Co., is seen here soon after delivery in 1868. These engines were the most attractive of the Craven goods and could easily be distinguished from their predecessors by the deep slotted frames, the polished brass dome cover and the bent over weatherboard. The locomotive was renumbered 469 in 1881 and withdrawn in 1894.

Like so many of these early LB&SCR engines, No.4 had a most complicated history. Originally built in 1861 as a 4-4-0T, it was rebuilt almost immediately as a 2-2-2ST. In this form, it was used on the Uckfield and Littlehampton branches before being renewed as a 2-4-0ST in January 1869. The photograph was taken at Battersea shed between then and 1873 when it was renumbered. It suffered two more renumberings before being scrapped in 1882.

A wash drawing by L.E. Brailsford of Croydon, founder member of the Stephenson Locomotive Society and a great Brighton enthusiast, depicting No.131, one of six tank engines built in 1858 for the West End and Crystal Palace line. Built as No.12, it was a well tank with inside and outside frames. These engines were unsuccessful in that they were rough riding and their tanks leaked. Most of the class were rebuilt: No.131 was rebuilt as a side tank in 1868 and lasted in this form until 1889.

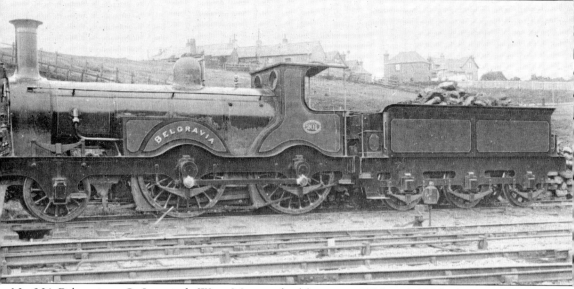

No.201 *Belgravia* at St Leonards West Marina shed between 1892 and 1896 when it was allocated there for working London Bridge semi-fasts. Built in 1871, it was one of six engines designed by Stroudley to work the heaviest expresses. Near the end of its days (it was withdrawn in 1899), the engine's paintwork is well worn.

Marking the transition from Craven to Stroudley, No.373 was one of a pair of what were intended to be double-framed saddle tanks ordered by Craven shortly before his resignation. They emerged from Brighton Works in 1871 as Nos 18 and 21 with single frames and the round topped tanks later to become so familiar on Stroudley's locomotives. In appearance they were a precursor of the D class, but not very effective. For this reason they were withdrawn after a relatively short existence. The locomotive was photographed between 1881, when it was renumbered, and 1886.

A singular conveyance, William Stroudley's delightful *Inspector* at Brighton, Lovers Walk in 1890. It entered service as a 2-4-0T built by Sharp Stewart in 1869 and numbered 96. In 1872, Stoudley transformed its appearance by providing his standard pattern of cab, a dome and a particularly handsome tall, copper-capped chimney. Sadly Stroudley died before he could see its final metamorphosis into his personal inspection saloon complete with speaking tube to the cab. After completion by Billinton as No.481, it entered service in 1890 and was used for a few years before withdrawal in 1898.

Arguably, the most celebrated engines to be designed by Stroudley were the A class, today called 'Terriers' but better known in their heyday as 'Rooters'. No.42 *Tulsehill* was built in 1877 and scrapped in 1925. Allocated to Midhurst shed when photographed at Brighton being coupled to a carriage truck bearing a trap, and a horsebox whose owner may be identified on the original print as Young.

The Woodside and South Croydon Railway was a joint line with the South Eastern Railway opened in 1885. Never a success, it closed in 1983. The branch service headed by Terrier No.82 *Boxhill* is depicted at the Selsdon end of Woodside Station soon after the opening of the line at a time when the service was worked in alternate years by the respective companies. The engine still survives, beautifully restored, at the National Railway Museum. Photograph by Phillips of the Oxford House Studios, Croydon.

When Stroudley came to Brighton, one of his first tasks was to design a new goods locomotive. The result was the powerful C class of which twenty were built, two in 1871 and the remainder in 1873-1874. They were nicknamed 'Jumbos' after the famous elephant in London Zoo. No.403 stands in Norwood Junction yard on 6 July 1898 in a photograph by F.H. Schove. It was scrapped in 1902. The leading brake van, No.244, is of the R.J. Billinton pattern introduced in 1894 and has the shaded lettering used on Brighton goods stock in the 1880s and 1890s.

Twelve more 0-6-0s were built as Nos.421-432 of the C1 Class, being a development of the C Class. No.432, built in 1887 and withdrawn in 1910, stands at Fratton shed. The class had the reputation of being sluggish with heavy fuel and water consumption. With two exceptions, all of them had gone by 1911.

Stroudley built fourteen D Class (later D2 Class) 0-4-2 tender engines for mixed traffic work as a development of his successful D Class tanks. The first of the class, No.300 *Lyons* of September 1876 was photographed by T. Chambers of Portsmouth at Fratton shed in 1901. It had a Craven tender on that occasion but was fitted with a Stroudley outside framed tender shortly before withdrawal in 1903. The photographer has nicely captured the sanding and the glint of the low sun on the tender.

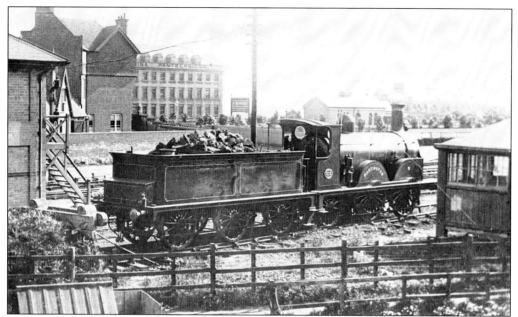

No.212 *Hartington* in a well composed photograph by Dr T.F. Budden at St Leonards West Marina. Built in 1880, the engine was in a small class of six that were in many respects the precursors of the 'Gladstones'. The photograph was taken between 1891 and 1897. The back of St Leonards East Signal Box, opened in 1891 and closed in 1928, is visible behind the engine while features of note in the background include the Marina Pantechnicon furniture depository, the enormous sign erected by the railway to publicize its services and the company's stables put up in 1886.

In the early 1890s, a representative of Stroudley's celebrated B or 'Gladstone' class, No.186 *De La Warr*, is posed with its crew at Newhaven Harbour in front of the company's highly distinctive bonded warehouse built in 1890.

Pullmans were more closely associated with the LB&SCR than any other company. Here a down Pullman express is drawn by the 1889 Paris Exhibition award winner, B Class No.189 *Edward Blount*, named after the great financier and Chairman of the Western Railway of France whose home was at Brambletye near East Grinstead. It is a wet winter day and the location is south of Patcham tunnel. The leading vehicle is 'Pullman Pup' van No.29, built in 1895 and used for generating electricity for lighting the Pullmans. Photograph by Dr T.F. Budden.

Photographs of trains in motion on the eastern part of the coast line are surprisingly rare. Dr Budden captured No.218 *Beaconsfield* near Cooden *c*.1896. The train comprises oil-lit Stroudley stock including a luggage van and a straight-sided brake van built in the early 1870s. The body of one of these was discovered in excellent condition at Fittleworth in the 1980s and has been preserved.

In the early 1900s, the LB&SCR conducted experiments with oil burning and No.198 *Sheffield* (named after Lord Sheffield of Sheffield Park) was fitted in September 1902 with Johnson's patent vaporizer burner. The company had hoped to make use of cheap oil from the Crowborough area but the experiment was not a success and all the engines converted to burn oil were reconverted to coal burning, No.198 being altered in December 1904. Photographed at Brighton, it has the continuous handrail running round the smoke box applied on re-boilering in 1902.

In the eyes of many observers, Stroudley's G class singles were the most attractive of all his designs. No.345 *Plumpton* at Brighton in the early 1890s photographed by G.B. Spencer Johnstone.

D1 No.261 *Wigmore* in suburban service on the South London line, *c.*1904. Comprising 125 locomotives, Stroudley's D1s were numerically the largest single class in the south of England and many enjoyed long lives, *Wigmore* built in 1882 lasting until 1938.

A typical suburban train of the period 1880 to 1910, D1 No.230 *Brookhouse* on a 10 coach close coupled set of Stroudley four wheel carriages near Balham Intermediate signal box. This was a favourite haunt of the photographer Dr T.F. Budden, who probably took this view in 1902. Such trains represented the less than glamorous nature of many of the company's services.

The standard Stroudley goods tank was the E1 class, one of which, No.144 *Chambery*, stands at Battersea shed in 1882 for its photograph to be taken by the pioneer railway photographer R.H. Bleasdale. Bleasdale took a number of broadside views at this location in the years 1881-1882. The E1s were named after what must have seemed very exotic places on the Continent and were painted in the goods green although some carried passenger livery in the 1880s when there was a shortage of passenger locomotives. No.144 was built in 1879 and was withdrawn in 1936.

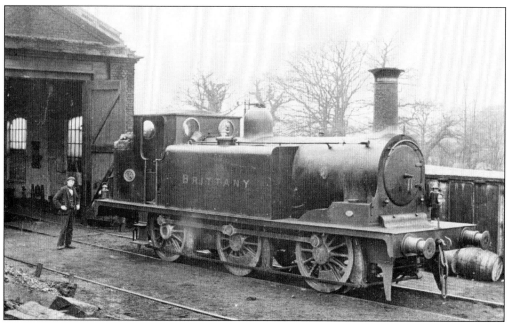

E1 No.104 *Brittany* is seen in original condition looking a little shabby at the old shed at Three Bridges. Prior to the line widening of 1907, this was situated at a lower level than the station on the up side of the line. Built in 1876, No.104 was one of ten converted in the 1920s to radial tanks as E1R for use in the west country and lasted in this form until 1956.

The unique 'E Special' No.157 *Barcelona* at Eastbourne, c.1905. Leaves on the line are today often perceived to be a problem but No.157 was built in 1884 to deal with just such a difficulty. The Cuckoo line from Eridge to Hailsham had opened in 1880 and problems were being experienced with slipping in wet weather and leaf fall time. No.157 spent the first twenty years of its existence on the daily Eastbourne to Tunbridge Wells goods service. Surprisingly, it was rarely photographed, only three views being known although it was not withdrawn until 1922.

D3 Class 0-4-4T No.390 *St Leonards* in the sylvan setting of the old Three Bridges locomotive yard. The unusually light rendering of the Stroudley passenger livery was probably the result of the use of an early panchromatic plate. These engines were a development of the Midland Railway 0-4-4Ts and No.390, which was built in 1894, was not withdrawn until 1955, the last survivor of the class by some two years. This class had a particularly handsome chimney which was faired into the smoke box in such a way that the join was indiscernible.

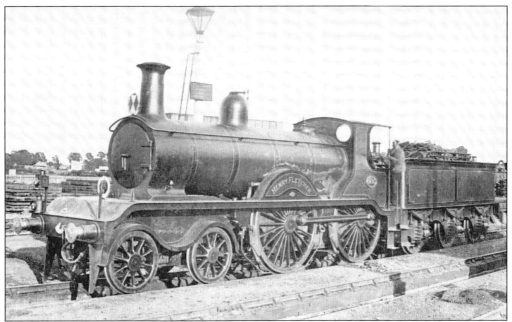

R.J. Billinton intended his B Bogie (later B2) class of 4-4-0 to take over from the 'Gladstones' on the some of the principal expresses but their boilers were simply too small. They were soon relegated to secondary workings. It has to be said though that they were beautifully proportioned engines and had a purity of line that the larger and infinitely more capable B4s never quite achieved, handsome engines though they were. No.203 *Henry Fletcher* stands at Fratton shed with much of the paint on the boiler burnt off. Built in 1897, it was rebuilt as a B2X in 1909 and scrapped in 1930.

No.213 *Bessemer* on the down Sunday 'Pullman Limited' passing the old station at Thornton Heath on 23 October 1898. It was the last B2 and emerged from Brighton Works late in 1897 with a larger boiler than its predecessors. Classified B3 by Marsh, it showed little advance in terms of power and, following rebuilding in 1908, it was no longer distinguishable from the other B2s. The photograph is by P.J. Mullett.

The practice of panning (moving the camera to keep the subject sharp while showing movement to give an impression of speed) was rare in pre-grouping days. The first photographer to use the technique is believed to have been P.W. Pilcher in 1889 but it was not common until the 1950s. This view of No.213 *Bessemer* taken near Nonsuch Park, Cheam, in 1907 is a fine example.

One of Billinton's capable B4s, No.61 *Ladysmith* in original form with the distinctive safety valves known to contemporaries as 'bathing drawers'. The location is Victoria during rebuilding with a temporary canopy prominent behind the engine.

Billinton's goods locomotive, the Class C2, was very much in the Derby small engine tradition. It steamed well but was less powerful than its Stroudley predecessors and many of the class were re-boilered from 1908 onwards. Often called 'Vulcans' because they were built by the Vulcan Foundry, they were often used on excursions in the summer as seen here. No.544, which was built in 1901 and rebuilt as a C2X in 1911, carries the double diamond special head-code. It has had coal rails added but is otherwise in original condition.

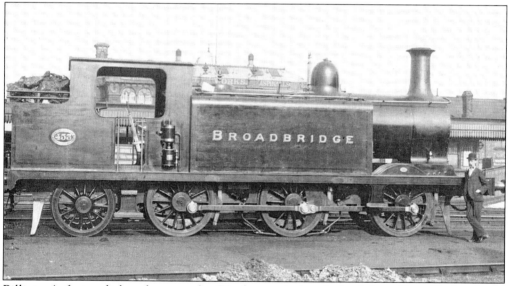

Billinton's first radial tanks were the E3 class, a design derived from Stroudley's solitary 'West Brighton'. Handsome in goods green livery, No.453 *Broadbridge* stands in front of the New Cross locomotive sheds with the ornate building constructed for the diary firm Letts but used by this time as Aspinall's Enamel Works forming the background as it did for so many LB&SCR locomotive portraits.

Seen south of Dorking, E3 No.165 (ex *Blatchington*) in goods black on a ballast train comprising two of the distinctive Stroudley brake vans and eight three plank ballast wagons of the LB&SCR's standard design used from 1905 onwards. Photograph by H. Gordon Tidey.

No.509 *Southover*, a Billinton radial tank of class E4 built in 1900, passes Hove West signal box with a train comprising Stroudley four wheelers and a Billinton six wheel third as second vehicle. The E4s were extensively used for suburban and local work.

Billinton's E5 class were widely used on express and local duties. Here is No.589 *Ambersham* at the same location on a west bound coast line train. A young woman with a large hat is leaning out of a most interesting vehicle, a Stroudley 26ft Second Class saloon, believed to be one of six built to diagram 23 in 1881-1882.

Excursion traffic was a major source of income to the LB&SCR. Happy excursionists lean out of the windows as E5 No.568 *Carisbrooke* passes through the LSWR station at Epsom in 1906. The second vehicle is a six wheeled Stroudley saloon of a type much favoured for this traffic. LSWR close coupled stock of the 1870s stands in the background.

No.416 of class E6, the small wheeled derivative of the E5s intended for goods work, takes a goods train through Wallington, *c*.1919, in an early photograph by O.J. Morris.

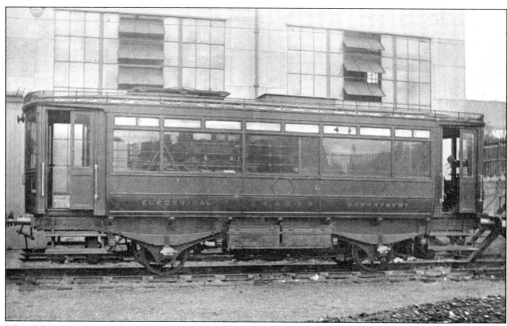

The LB&SCR introduced two petrol railcars in 1905. Both were built by Dick Kerr and fitted with Daimler engines. No.4 was used between Eastbourne and St Leonards and on the Kemp Town and Seaford branches before its lack of reliability led to its removal from passenger service. From September 1912, it became Electrical Department No.4 and was used to inspect and repair overhead wiring on the 'Elevated Electrics' in which guise it is seen here at Peckham Rye car sheds in 1913.

Five

Locomotives:
The Marsh and Lawson
Billinton Era

Marsh H1 Atlantic No.41 at Victoria, c.1908. The picture displays one of the features of the rebuilt station: the centre roads made it possible for incoming locomotives to exit the station prior to the removal of the carriages. Photograph from the Pouteau Collection.

The H2s ordered by Billinton in 1911 while Marsh was on sick leave had larger cylinders than their predecessors, while externally the most noticeable difference was the straight rather than stepped running plate. This study by F.E. Mackay shows No.423 leaving Victoria with the 5.45 to Worthing, c.1915.

Douglas Earle Marsh, who had previously been employed at Doncaster, introduced his own version of Ivatt's 4-4-2T design in 1906 as the I1 class. However, they proved to be dismal performers and were rebuilt by the Southern Railway. No.604, built in 1907, displays its modified E5 chimney as it stands at Lewes.

In contrast, the larger boiler of the I2 class is apparent on No.12, also at Lewes in 1913. The ten members of the class proved little better than the I1s.

Marsh finally succeeded with the handsome I3s of which No.23 is seen on a Pullman express near Lewes in 1913. This was the engine involved in the trials with the London & North Western Railway in 1909 which proved the value of superheating to that company.

Marsh's attempt at producing a powerful goods locomotive, the C3 class, was unsuccessful and the engines were largely used on local work. No.303 on a goods near Arundel, c.1920. Other than Stroudley brake van 217, all the vehicles are private owners or other companies' stock.

In the first decade of the twentieth century, the 'Terriers' found a new role on motor trains. No.667 (originally No.67 *Brixton*) was converted in 1907 and is seen coupled to one of Earle Marsh's 'Balloon' trailer third brakes from the second batch built to diagram 180 in 1906. The location is believed to be on the Oxted line.

The first member of the B class, No.214 *Gladstone* itself, is at East Croydon in Marsh umber as fitted with Marsh boiler and Doncaster-type safety valves. The different profile to the lower part of the cab that distinguished No.214 from the remainder of the class is apparent. Photograph from a quarter plate glass negative in my collection, one of a number of views mostly taken at East Croydon and formerly belonging to J.N. Maskelyne.

No.289 (ex *Holmbury*) at Horsham, *c*.1922. From 1905, the D tanks were fitted with motor train equipment, No.289 being so equipped in 1917. It carries a Marsh boiler. Horsham South Signal Box was built to Saxby and Farmer design in 1875 in a manner that harked back to the tall boxes of the 1860s with exposed framing. Shored up by baulks of timber, it managed to last until replaced in connection with the Mid-Sussex electrification in April 1938.

D1 No.79 was rebuilt by Marsh in 1910 with a high pitched boiler. It was not a great success and remained the only member of Class D1X. Following renumbering as No.349 in June 1913, it is seen at East Croydon.

In contrast to the dismal B2, the B4 class was a great success from its introduction in 1899. No.43 (ex *Duchess of Fife*) in Marsh condition with flared cast iron chimney, exhaust steam ejectors and equalising bars on the springs poses for the camera of E.S. Hallett, a fine photographer of the LB&SCR in the Edwardian period whose negatives are sadly lost. This card was sent by him on 11 May 1910 and he wrote on the reverse: 'Hope you will like this photo of I. Clarke and 43. I took it last Monday afternoon at Three Bridges. I also got a ripping one of Packham at Haywards Heath on Tuesday which I will send later. Coming back by stopping train with Clarke on Monday, we ran from Balcombe – H.H. 3 7/8 miles in 5.36, start to stop. Max 59.2.'

Miraculously, here is the 'ripping' photograph Hallett referred to in his postcard. No.47 (ex *Canada*) has the Marsh boiler that was fitted in March 1908 and Driver Packham and his fireman pose by their engine. Hallett sent the card on 12 May, writing: 'Here is the one of Packham. I had to get the loco in this position as the light was bad and I only had 2 minutes in which to put my camera up and take it. I don't think it is so bad. Had another good run with this loco and driver Tuesday last week. Will tell you about it when I write next.'

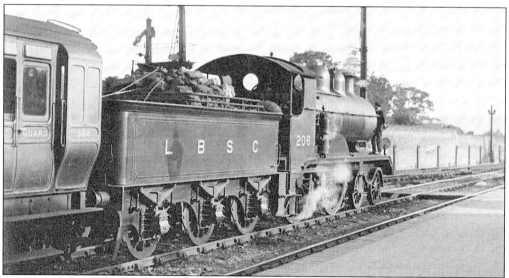

Marsh had contemplated scrapping the B2s but instead decided to fit them with the boiler he designed for the C3 goods from 1907. The result was a useful locomotive for secondary services. No.206 (ex *Smeaton*) waits to move off one summer's evening at Horsham. The second dome is for L. Billinton's top feed apparatus, the new boiler being fitted in January 1922. Rear views were frowned upon by the cognoscenti but they do make a change from the ever present front three-quarter picture.

The B2Xs looked well from the rear. No.317 stands at East Croydon, *c.*1910 following rebuilding in 1908. Print from a glass plate in my collection.

Four of the E4s were fitted by Marsh with his I2 boiler, the resultant engines being known as Class E4X. The effect was not altogether happy as the squat boiler mountings and the extended smoke box seemed out of proportion with the cab and tanks of what was originally a harmonious design. No.477 (ex *Poynings*) seen at East Croydon, was rebuilt in April 1911. It has received tapered buffers and a riveted buffer-beam.

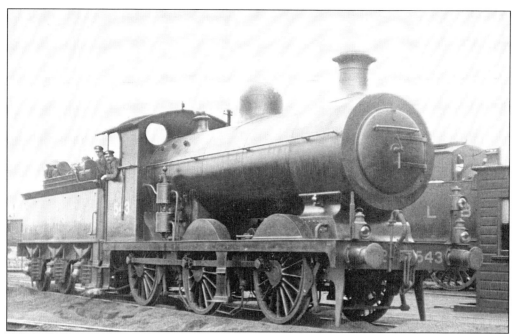

While the C3s were unsuccessful, Marsh's fitting of the same boiler to the C2 produced the excellent C2X class. No.543 was rebuilt in 1915 and lasted until 1960.

A Phoenix super-heater was fitted to B4 No.59 in May 1912. The cost was considerable and the engine needed constant attention so its removal in December 1915 was of little surprise. The ungainly proportions of the new smoke box are graphically displayed in this view at Lewes soon after rebuilding.

B4 No.44 equipped for royal duties at Brighton. Additional fittings include a crown, the special royal headlamps and headcode discs and coats of arms. The engine is as fitted in December 1921 with a new Robinson superheated boiler with an extended smoke box, Weir feed pump and new 20in cylinders.

Marsh's swansong was a supremely elegant design: No.325 *Abergavenny* was built in 1910 and is seen here at New Cross, *c.*1920. The engine has the oval buffers fitted in 1919 and its buffer beam has been trimmed to improve clearances.

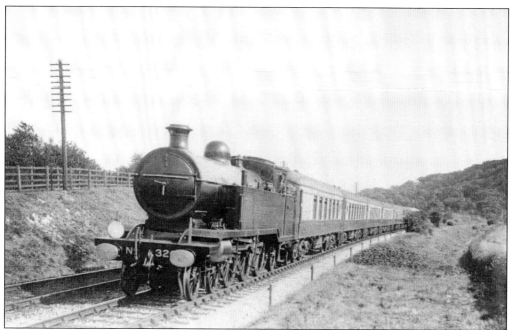

Marsh's handsome 4-6-2T No.326 *Bessborough* which was completed by Billinton on the up 'Southern Belle' north of Patcham Tunnel. Photograph by T.B. Welch, *c*.1922.

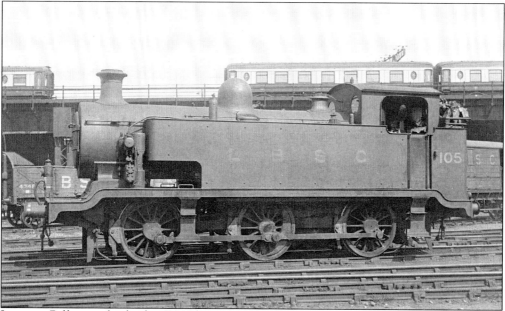

Lawson Billinton built the E2 Class to replace some of the Stroudley E1s. The first five appeared in 1913-1914 and a second batch of five, Nos 105-109, were completed in 1915-1916. They had a particularly neat outline while the second series had extended tanks as is evident in J.N. Maskelyne's photograph of No.105 at Battersea shed on 17 May 1924. The vehicles in the background are of interest: on the right one of the LB&SCR's final design of brake van, No.393 built in 1923 and the Pullman *Bessborough* from the 1908 'Southern Belle' set.

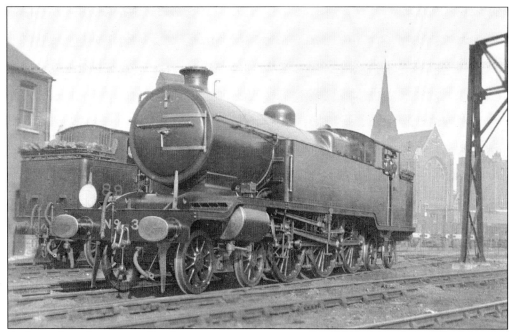

Perhaps the ultimate in Brighton motive power were Billinton's splendid Baltic tanks. No.329 *Stephenson*, so named after lobbying from the Stephenson Locomotive Society, most of whose early members displayed an enthusiasm for the LB&SCR akin to fanaticism, stands by the turntable at Victoria in 1921 for this portrait by A.B. MacLeod.

Baltic No.327 *Charles C. Macrae* at South Croydon on the 3.10 p.m. down 'Southern Belle' which includes second class cars and the solitary elliptical roof brake van No.191 built to diagram No.234 in 1907. Photograph by F.E. Mackay.

Billinton's most successful design was the K Class mogul introduced in 1913. No.346, which was built three years later, waits resplendent in the goods black livery at Fratton on a passenger working. Although designed for goods work, the Ks were true mixed traffic locomotives and were frequently employed on passenger duties. The entire class of seventeen engines was summarily withdrawn in December 1962. Photograph by O.J. Morris.

Another K, No.340, is seen ex-works at Brighton in May 1922 after being fitted with a Worthington-Simpson pump and feed water system. It was not a great success and the locomotive only ran in this form until December 1923. Photograph by T.B. Welch.

Billinton made a number of experiments with patent devices. K class No.351 was fitted with a Lewis Draft Appliance and stovepipe chimney in April 1921. The latter did nothing for its appearance as is seen in this rare view by T.B. Welch of it in service in 1921 in red oxide livery without lettering.

Twelve of the E4 class were sent to France late in 1917 to join the Railway Operating Division. Only two photographs of them in the dull khaki livery of the ROD are known. This one depicts No.562 soon after its return in March 1919.

Twelve of the B4s were rebuilt between 1922 and 1924 by L. Billinton as Class B4X. The first rebuild No.55 (ex *Emperor*) was photographed by H.M. Madgwick on 22 August 1922 at Worthing while undergoing trials in shop grey. The rebuilds which were fitted with the superheated K class boiler never came up to expectations due largely to erratic steaming.

Even at the close of the LB&SCR's existence, the Gladstones could still be seen on front line duties. No.199 *Samuel Laing* works hard as it hauls an up train north of Patcham Tunnel, *c.*1922. It still carried a Stroudley boiler, although later modifications visible include a Marsh chimney and smoke box door hinges, dual braking and tender coal guards. Photograph by H. Gordon Tidey.

Six

People

The staff at Polegate with carriage destination boards acting as a title.

William Stroudley (1833-1889), a portrait by W.&A.H. Fry of Brighton, believed to be previously unpublished. Depictions of the great locomotive engineer who served the LB&SCR from 1870 until his death are rare. His obituary in *The Engineer* declared that he had 'an intense and truly refined sense of mechanical fitness. On him a faulty, ill-designed, or unmeaning detail had the same effects as a discord on a musician.'

Samuel Laing (1812-1897), 'the Infant Samuel' from the Spy cartoon in *Vanity Fair* of 16 August 1873. One of the most significant railway chairmen of the Victorian age, Laing rescued the company twice. Other aspects of the career of this remarkable polymath included politics (acting as Finance Minister for India), administration (as a civil servant in the railway department of the Board of Trade), business (as Chairman of the Crystal Palace Company and the General Credit and Discount Company) and writing (as a best selling author of popular scientific works and even a novel).

John Peake Knight (1828-1886), the LB&SCR's General Manager was another highly talented man. He invented the world's first traffic signals which were introduced in 1868, an event commemorated by a green plaque placed at 12 Bridge Street, Westminster. This is the only known illustration of him other than a cartoon that appeared in *The Brightonian*. Engraving by courtesy of the Knight family.

In the early years of the twentieth century, there was a revival of interest in rural life and the old Sussex country folk were regarded as being especially 'picturesque' and were much favoured by the producers of picture postcards. Under the sentimental title 'Old Friends' an agricultural worker holding milk cans and a locally made Sussex trug poses with an LB&SCR porter.

A group of LB&SCR guards. The location is unknown.

Platelayers out on the line near Offham, north of Lewes.

A Sunday gang putting in the new cross-over road at Thornton Heath on 12 August 1900, with an assortment of goods stock including Brighton Open As, a Midland Railway open, a Great Eastern Railway van and private owner wagons.

Seven

Traffic:
Ordinary and Special

Stroudley Third No.1090 built close-coupled in 1881 for suburban services. It is typical of the rather spartan accommodation provided for third class passengers with narrow compartments and only low partitions between them. It forms one of a series of official photographs taken at Lovers Walk, Brighton by the Electrical Department in 1882-1883.

By way of contrast, main line composite No.145 of 1877 displays the superior compartment widths. The grain of the varnished mahogany livery is brought out particularly well.

Stroudley horse box No.130, built in 1874 and photographed at Brighton Lovers Walk, another in the series of official views taken under the auspices of the company's Electrical Department in 1882-1883.

94

Where the Brighton company really fell down was in the absence of corridor stock. Other than Pullmans, only one corridor set ran on the LB&SCR, three coaches built in 1907 for the prestigious 'City Limited' businessmen' express. Seen here, c.1920, saloon first brake 31, parlour saloon first 152 and corridor lavatory first 151 head the train. The latter two carriages display the 'clipper' profile resulting from their 9ft width. Photograph by C. Laundy.

The epitome of luxury – the 1908 'Southern Belle' which 'suggests to the imaginative traveller the annexe of some sumptuous hotel which has taken flight by rail' in the words of the LB&SCR's publicists. This is the buffet car *Grosvenor*, panelled in Spanish mahogany and upholstered in green morocco.

Pullman Third Class car No.21 at East Croydon in 1924. The K-type car was built by the Midland Railway Carriage & Wagon Co. on the underframe of a former Great Western Railway ambulance carriage and entered service in February 1922. It was scrapped in 1943 following air raid damage at the Preston Park Pullman works. Photograph by O.J. Morris.

Battersea Wharf, one of the company's two principal London goods depots, c.1905. Lighters occupy the foreground while the main line out of Victoria runs on the embankment in the background. Battersea Pier Junction signal box, a tall cabin of 1865, is just above the large signboard while lines of sheeted Open As occupy the sidings. This is the only known view of the timber goods shed of 1866 which was replaced by a large brick structure in 1906.

Willow Walk, the most important of the London depots, was greatly enlarged at the turn of the twentieth century. A large new goods shed for outwards traffic was erected to the south of the Upper Grange Road over-bridge. Authorized in 1899, it was completed in 1903 and is seen here in a photograph by H. Gordon Tidey, c.1912.

The sorting sidings off the old alignment at Lewes, c.1908. The identities of the staff are unfortunately unkown. The view provides an excellent glimpse of No.7192, a standard Billinton cattle van distinguished from its Stroudley predecessors by the higher pitch of its roof.

97

The extensive marshalling sidings known as Upper Goods were a notable feature on the approach to Brighton Station. A B4-hauled up express with a Billinton double-ended brake leading passes a line of Stroudley brake vans, c.1908.

A goods hauled by C2X No.554 approaches the north end of Lewes tunnel, c.1920.

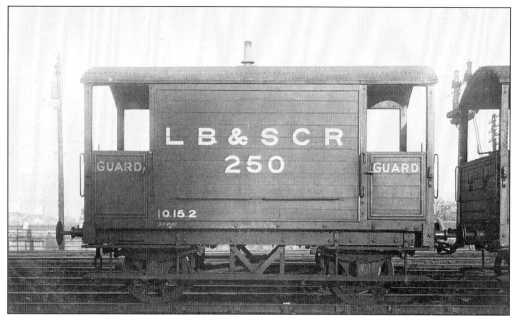

Billinton ten-ton brake van No.250, one of many built to diagram 22 between 1894 and 1907. It bears a paint date of 9 October 1907. Among the chalked destinations visible on the original print is Lillie Bridge, one of the principal handover points for cross-London traffic. Photographed at Brighton Upper Goods.

Bridge renewals taking place on the main line between Selhurst and Thornton Heath in 1896 prior to widening. A temporary ground frame for wrong line working has been set up and two signalmen are standing by it. A slotted post signal is behind them while on the right the girders are supported on three dumb-buffered, single bolster wagons.

The LB&SCR, through its connection to the South Railway Jetty at Portsmouth, was associated with the arrivals and departures of many notable figures. On 26 June 1913, President Poincaré of France inspects the Guard of Honour prior to joining the LB&SCR Royal Train for the trip to Victoria.

H1 Atlantic No.38 crosses the the bridge leading from the South Railway Jetty as it departs with the Royal Train. The naval dockyard is visible in the background.

The LB&SCR Royal Train headed by B4 No.42 *His Majesty* stands at the old Victoria in August 1902 awaiting the arrival of the Prince and Princess of Wales to convey them to Portsmouth for an Imperial tour. Robert Billinton is beside the engine and J.J. Richardson, the London District Superintendent is to his left. On the footplate is Driver Pullen. O.J. Morris copied a portion of this photograph but this is the first time it has been reproduced in its entirety from a framed original in my collection.

Another frequent outing for the Royal Train was to the races at Epsom. I2 No.15 passes Belmont as it takes King Edward VII down the Epsom Downs branch. The engine bears the handsome crest, which still exists today at the National Railway Museum, and a crown on the top lamp iron.

Decoration of locomotives for the excursions from London to Eastbourne in aid of the Station Masters and Inspectors' Mutual Aid and Widows Fund became an art form. Rivalry between Battersea and New Cross sheds, who prepared the engines for the Victoria and London Bridge trains respectively, was intense. Complete with carpet bedding and bust of Queen Victoria, B2 No.203 *Henry Fletcher* stands at New Cross in the jubilee year of 1897. Even the double diamond head-code disc is adorned and combined with the London Bridge board. The buildings visible are among the oldest part of the New Cross complex dating back to London and Croydon days.

Intruder in the camp. A B4 is entering Paddington on the short-lived through service between Brighton and the Great Western Railway terminus, which only ran from 1906 to 1907. A.F. Selby was one of the few people to photograph it and it is a shame that his photographs that day were not very successful.

In 1915, the company converted a number of the elliptical roofed carriages into two ambulance trains, one of which is posed at Lovers Walk, Brighton with No.326 *Bessborough*. The carriages concerned did not return to service but most of the underframes were reused.

A delightful scene at the level crossing north of Newhaven Town Station as the celebrated Terrier No.72 *Fenchurch* passes a Sussex cart. The view is probably after the sale of the engine to the Newhaven Harbour Company in 1898 as it retained full Stroudley livery. The Stroudley brake van used in ballast train service bears both the company's initials and the so-called illiterate mark.

By contrast, Woodgate Crossing near Barnham is seen, c.1920, with a B4 on an eastbound train. We are now firmly in the era of motor transport and the charabanc CD4683 of Southdown Motor Services, so long associated with LB&SCR territory, waits to cross.

Eight

Signal Boxes, Engine Sheds and Brighton Works

Patcham, a Saxby and Farmer box opened in 1868 and seen here shortly before closure in 1932. With their low pitched roofs, small window frames and generally squat appearance, these early boxes were most distinctive.

Merton Park, the junction of the LSWR/LB&SCR joint line from Tooting and the branch from West Croydon, showing the alley from Kingston Road flanked by the tall signal box of 1868 which was one of the oldest boxes in the London area when replaced on 28 August 1912.

Wandsworth Common which was unusual on the Brighton system in being mounted high over a running line. Photographed in May 1906, it was replaced on the widening of the line the following year.

Streatham signal box, *c.*1910, an example of what was the most common type of box to be found on the LB&SCR, the Saxby and Farmer design termed 5 by the Signalling Record Society. It was built in 1885 and closed in 1952.

A most handsome design of signal box was designed to complement the Myres stations, complete with tiled rather than slated roof, iron decorations along the ridge and elaborate timber framing. This is Singleton North box nearing completion in 1881, one of two boxes serving the extensive station laid out to serve Goodwood race traffic. Both boxes were abolished in 1933.

The standard LB&SCR design of the twentieth century with its gabled roof, Folly Hill replaced an earlier box in 1908 and lasted until the Brighton electrification of 1933. The card was sent by one of the soldiers depicted guarding the box who wrote: 'This the signal box to which we patrol. We saw a Red Cross train yesterday with the wounded inside. The doors were open but they would not talk much.'

The Brighton South box of 1882 which, with its 240-lever frame, was one of the largest on the Brighton system.

The interior of the old Thornton Heath signal box of 1872, photographed in 1897, showing the original twelve-lever Saxby and Farmer tappet frame. The box was pulled down on 21 June 1903 with the widening of the line and replaced by a sixty-four-lever box that lasted until 1976.

An early view of the Brighton sheds with, on the left, Stroudley 2-4-0 *Belgravia* or *Goodwood*, in original form with Adams safety valves, and, on the right, a Craven 2-2-2 believed to be one of Nos 10, 23, 32 or 41 of the 'Jenny Lind' type built in 1853-1854 at Brighton Works, the last of which was scrapped in 1877. A pair of open-slatted coke wagons dating back to 1851 stand alongside the primitive coaling stage.

The view of the Brighton engine sheds from Howard Place high on the chalk cliff above the station was a popular subject for photographers. The variety of motive power on shed that can be identified includes D1 No.249 *Hilsea*, B No.175 *Hayling*, D1 No.18 *Stockwell*, A No.642 *Tulsehill*, D3 No.384 *Cooksbridge*, D1 No.290 *Denbies*, B No.178 *Leatherhead*, D3 No.374 *Pulborough*, E4 No.581 *Warningcamp*, E4 No.475 *Partridge Green*, E5 No.593 *Hollington*, c.1905. In the background is Montpelier signal box and the sweep of the London Road viaduct.

New Cross, one of the two principal LB&SCR locomotive sheds in the London area, c.1904. Taken by W. Bennett, who is leaning over the fence of the up platform of New Cross Station, the picture shows, on the right, the 'Middle' shed of 1863 and, beyond it, the 'New' shed of 1882. B4 No.51 *Wolferton*, a C2 and a D1 can be clearly seen. An early arc lamp is in the background.

The LB&SCR was a line that engendered peculiar devotion from its many followers. The Stephenson Locomotive Society was formed in 1910. Although its brief extended to all companies, it was in its early days practically a Brighton locomotive fan club, prominent members including G.F. Burtt from the Brighton Drawing Office, J.N. Maskelyne, L.E. Brailsford and M.F. Long. Here a group of members pose by No.329 *Stephenson* at Battersea on a shed visit.

The carriage shop with an American-built Pullman receiving attention on the right. Billinton bogie stock is under construction while an inverted six wheel underframe is visible in the centre.

One of the two elliptical-roof trailer third brakes to diagram 179, known as 'balloons' on account of their roof profile, under construction at Brighton in 1905.

The paint shop on the west side of the main line. Carriages including bogie First No.145 receive the umber and cream livery introduced in 1905. The photograph gives a good view of an oil lamp housing and ventilators. The shop is lit by a myriad of low level gas jets to enable the painters to see what they are doing.

The boiler shop at Brighton Works, c.1910.

The steel roof for the new erecting shop at Brighton Works takes shape in 1908 high above the walls of the existing buildings dating back to the 1840s. Lines of Open As stand in the yard below.

The erecting shop after the 1908 rebuilding with its new steel trussed roof. The new thirty-five-ton overhead gantry crane built by Craven Bros is prominent. On the left are two I1s, the nearer being No.597.

Nine

A Brighton Railway Miscellany

A 'Goods Train Mishap' at Billingshurst on 1 October 1912. Such cards produced by local photographers are often the only visual record of minor accidents. A Great Eastern fitted van and a Midland Railway mineral wagon are among the casualties being removed by one of the LB&SCR's two fifteen-ton steam cranes built in 1898.

One of a number of cards issued by the local photographer H.H. Camburn showing the aftermath of Stroudley 0-6-0 No.423 falling into the turntable pit at Tunbridge Wells.

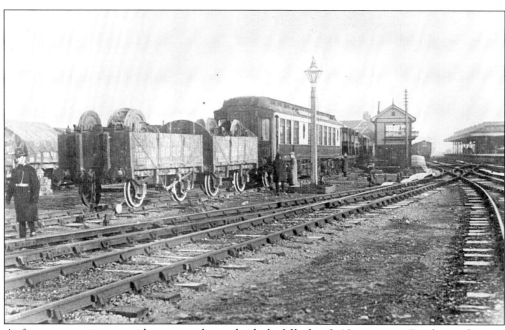

A far more serious accident was that which befell the 3.40 p.m. up Brighton fast on 29 January 1910 at Stoats Nest. Seven people died when one of the coaches derailed and mounted the platform at Stoats Nest Station. Some of the vehicles in the train including the Pullman 'Princess Patricia' of 1906 stand near the scene of the accident together with Open D 2929 and an Open A bearing wheels from the damaged vehicles.

The engineman's cap badge of the LB&SCR was a handsome thing of copper with a relief of D3 No.363 *Goldsmid*.

The company acquired four inspection cars. One of them is seen complete with head-code on the Hayling Island branch just to the south of Havant with the East Street bridge just visible in the background.

LB&SCR water columns could still be seen out of use thirty years ago. Distinguished by a plate with 'Brighton Works' and the date of construction cast into the column itself, this one is at Lewes in 1970.

The traditional railway seat was still to be found in large numbers until about twelve years ago when the remaining examples were replaced with the modern sheet metal design. The LB&SCR favoured two designs, that illustrated here at Hove in 1970 and a more curvaceous pattern.

An army of porters and vanguards are engaged in carrying boxes to the company's vans at London Bridge. LB&SCR van livery was distinctive in that the company styled itself 'South Coast Railway' with 'Portsmouth' and 'Hastings' boards prominent.

The SS *Dieppe* leaving Newhaven. A triple screw turbine ship built at the Fairfield yard at Govan, she was launched in 1905 and served the company until sale in 1933 for conversion into a private yacht. Her end came in 1941 when she was sunk off Tobruk.

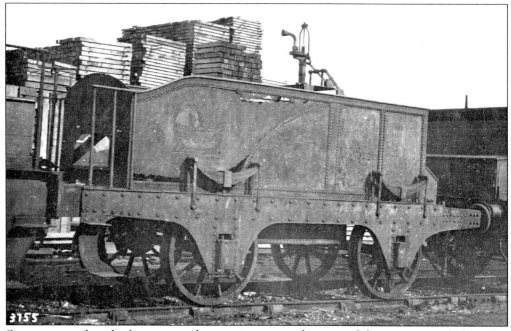

Some very early vehicles remained in service use at the turn of the century including this Sharp Roberts tender dating back to the 1840s.

One of a series of views taken in July 1908 to show the works for the electrification of the South London line or the 'Elevated Electric' as the LB&SCR called it in emulation of the American 'Els'. For part of its route, the line traversed LC&DR tracks. Looking towards Clapham Station with its tall Saxby and Farmer signal box, one can discern W.R. Sykes's signal works to the right of the station building.

Building the car sheds for the overhead electrics at Peckham Rye in 1908. A C2 waits with a line of opens to carry away spoil. The car sheds, which were built of corrugated iron, lasted until the early 1970s.

Tulse Hill goods yard located in the vee between the fork to West Norwood on the left and the line to Streatham in the centre. On the right is the spur to Leigham Junction. The yard was used principally for coal traffic. The photograph was one of a series taken to show the overhead electric installations for the electrification of 1912.

The car sheds for the electrified services at Selhurst nearing completion. The Brighton company much favoured corrugated iron for certain applications which were out of the view of the public. The structure survives today although threatened with demolition.

The LB&SCR was often under threat from those who wished to deprive it of its monopoly of the Brighton traffic seen as a honeypot by many other companies. Even as late as 1902, a London and Brighton Electric Railway was promoted and this artists impression from a brochure put out by the scheme's backers depicts the type of electric train we might have found on the Brighton service had they succeeded. The primitive streamlining has echoes of the famous 'Windcutters' of the PLM in France which were very much in vogue at the time.

Timetables changed greatly in appearance over the years. Early editions such as this example of May 1849 were small in size.

THE

LONDON, BRIGHTON & SOUTH COAST RAILWAY

MAY, 1849.

MAY, 1849.

TIME TABLES,

CONTAINING THE

DEPARTURE & ARRIVAL of TRAINS

TO AND FROM

London, Croydon, Epsom, Reigate, Horsham, Brighton, Lewes, Newhaven, Hastings, Arundel, Chichester, and Portsmouth, and the intermediate Stations.

Published by Authority of the Company.

LONDON:

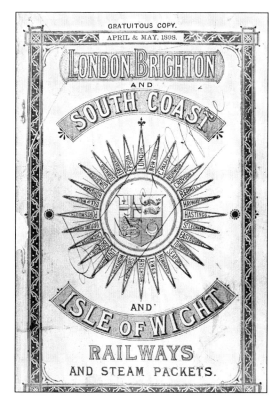

GRATUITOUS COPY.

APRIL & MAY, 1898.

LONDON, BRIGHTON

AND

SOUTH COAST

AND

ISLE OF WIGHT

RAILWAYS

AND STEAM PACKETS.

By 1898, the date of this issue, the format had become standardized with that of the other major British railways; a substantial foolscap sized volume with decorative covers. A version of the company's crest still forms the centrepiece of the design which takes the form of a sun with the principal destinations set out as sunbeams; somewhat crude but typical of many late nineteenth century graphics.

Separate continental timetables were issued. These were smaller in format than the general timetables and the covers varied in design over time. This one, from 1898, has most attractive coloured covers depicting one of the company's steamers (possibly the *Paris* or *Rouen* of 1888) approaching Newhaven. Subsequent issues had a plainer style with no illustration.

MENU

VICTORIA STATION
RESTAURANT

London, Brighton &
South Coast Railway

The LB&SCR had no clear house style for its publications. An Art Nouveau influence is apparent in this menu dated 8 January 1908 which offered a *table d'hôte* luncheon for two shillings.

The LB&SCR put out publicity material to encourage tourism but not as much as might be expected from a company whose fortunes were so bound up with the holiday trade. 'South Coast Holidays' was published in English, French and German in 1910 and commenced with a description of the 'Southern Belle': 'The finest train in the world now connects London with Brighton, its Sea-Suburb.'

An advertising postcard issued by W. Bennett, locomotive photographer of Hove, illustrates the considerable interest in collecting photographs of LB&SCR engines as early as the 1900s. Photographs of Stroudley were available for the cognoscenti. Many of Bennett's plates still exist in a number of collections.

Between 1902 and 1904, the west siding at East Grinstead was used to store withdrawn locomotives awaiting scrapping. Many of the Stroudley engines withdrawn with the onset of new Billinton classes ended up here. Among the sorry looking examples with wheels and many fittings removed are Terrier No.656 *Shoreditch*, D3 No.612 *Hartington*, D1 No.3 *Battersea* and an unidentified C.

A young couple caught by the camera on 28 September 1913 as they make their way back to Brighton station, a journey familiar to millions of holidaymakers over the past 150 years and an appropriate end to this exploration of the LB&SCR.

Acknowledgements

The bulk of the photographs have come from my own collection. I owe a great debt to those who have allowed me to undertake the very enjoyable task of looking through their photographic collections: B.D. Howe, L.G. Marshall, R.C. Riley and A. Woodard. R. Blencowe, J.L. Smith of Lens of Sutton, R.S. Carpenter and K. Marx have kindly allowed me to reproduce photographs from their collections.

R. Blencowe Collection – 13(t)

R.S. Carpenter Collection – 99(b), 160(b)

B.D. Howe Collection – 44(b), 74(t

L.Marshall Collection – 12(b), 15(t), 17(b), 19(b), 22, 25, 27(b), 28(b), 31, 32(b), 34, 35, 39(b), 40(b), 41(t), 50(b), 84(b), 91(b), 95(b), 96(t), 97(b), 99(t), 112(b), 113(b), 114, 122(t)

R.C. Riley Collection – cover, 11, 14(b), 15(b), 16(t), 18, 28(t), 38(t), 45(b), 47(b), 48(b), 49, 50(t), 65(b), 72(b), 73, 79(b), 80(t), 81(t), 83(b), 84(t), 88, 92, 93, 94, 100(t), 104, 108(b), 109, 116(t), 120(b), 121

A. Woodard Collection – 48(t), 103(t)

Lens of Sutton – 19(t), 21, 36(b), 37(b), 38(b), 41(b), 42, 43, 44(t), 46(t), 70(t), 105, 115

Bluebell Archives – 20, 24, 61(b)

As always, I am indebted to the usual sources for factual details: Bradley and Burtt on locomotives, Newbury, Abson and Gould on coaching stock and Bixley, Blackburn, Chorley and King on goods vehicles. Architectural and signal box construction dates are derived from my own research in the LB&SCR's minute books at the Public Record Office, Kew, and the late J.M. Wagstaff's signalling records. Finally, I would like to give special thanks to E. Hart, formerly Secretary of the Brighton Circle, for checking the captions and proof-reading.